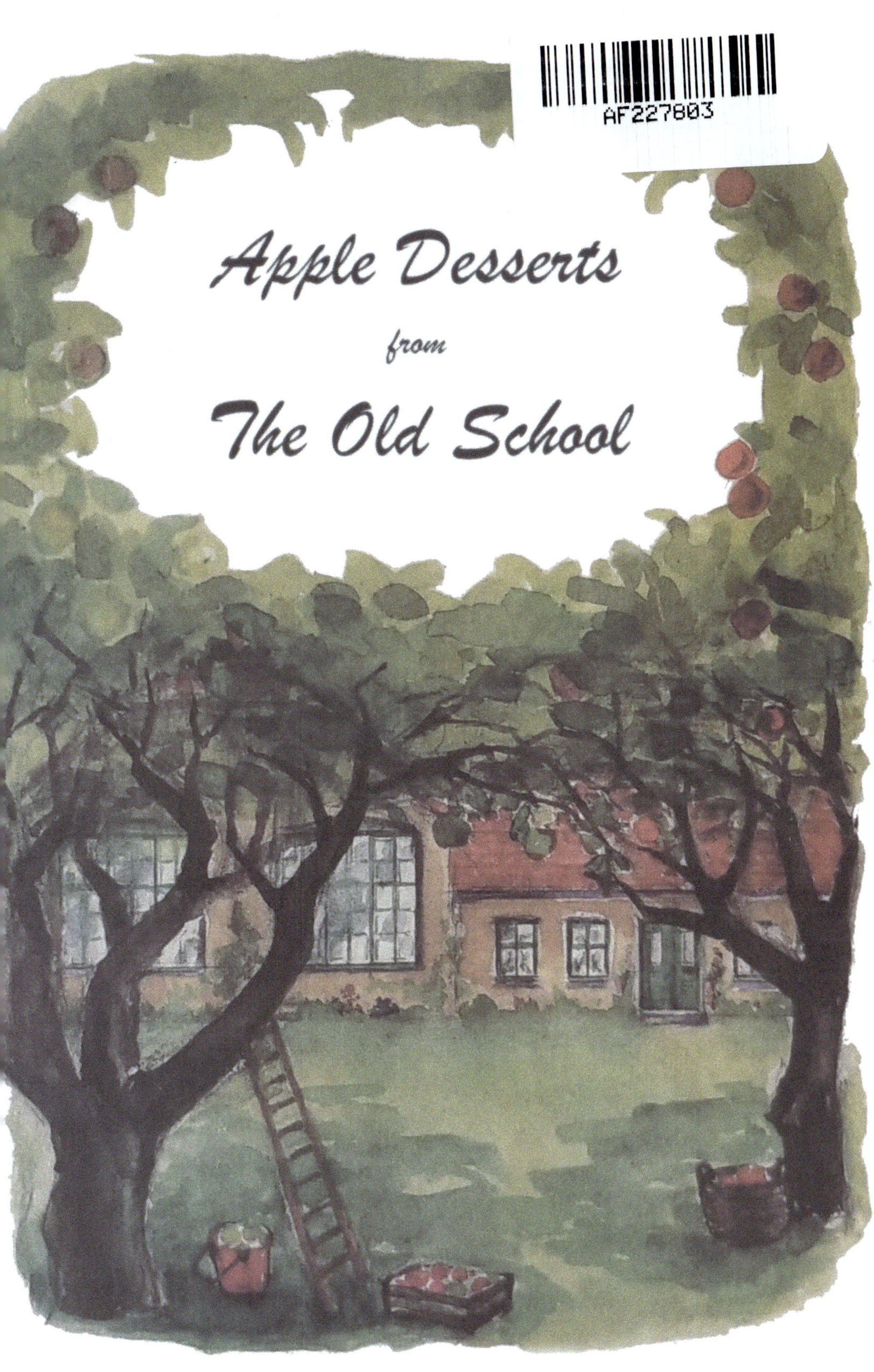

Apple Desserts

from

The Old School

Apple Desserts from The Old School

Copyright © 2021 by Inga Linde Jensen.

Paperback ISBN: 978-1-63812-028-5
Ebook ISBN: 978-1-63812-029-2

Published by Green Sage Agency   05/11/2021

Green Sage Agency
1-888-366-9989
inquiry@greensageagency.com

Apple Desserts

from

The Old School

*Written and Illustrated
by Inga Linde Jensen*

Note to the Reader:

Since this cook book was originally written in Danish, we have retained the original measurement units, but have also added measurement units more commonly used in the USA.

l means liters

dl means deciliters (one tenth of a liter)

g means grams

For reference the following approximate conversion chart is supplied:

1 l = 1 liter = 10 deciliters = 4¼ cups

1 dl = 1 deciliter = ½ cup

1 stick of butter = 113 grams of butter

125 g of butter = 1⅛ stick of butter = 4½ oz of butter

100 g of butter = 3½ oz of butter = ⅞ stick of butter

200 g = 7 oz

Written and illustrated by Inge Linde Jensen.

Translated by Ragnhild Munck.

An old garden with many apple trees, blooming in splendid beauty, bearing colorful fruits - and an old schoolhouse from 1842 — to which the garden belongs, give an impression of romantic rural idyll — and so it is.

There are many memories linked to this old country school house. Memories as prosaic as apple desserts.

Prosaic, yes and no! Do not apples and poetry always go together?

The fragrance alone!

And remember the apple used by Paris when pointing out the most beautiful of the three godesses — and the infamous apple which William Tell must shoot off the head of his son with bow and arrow.

Yes, the apple has played an important part in many stories as a symbol of both love and eternal youth — and so it does here in this school, now as before.

Many years ago this country school was closed in favor of the central school in town.

Happy are we who took over the old house from those families who were here as teachers and who were skilled as gardeners.

The trees they planted here bear witness to their wisdom and practical sense. So much thought has gone into their choice of fruit varieties, that we who live here now can harvest apples and other fruits from July and till frost hits the ground.

An old neighbor remembers when he attended school here about 80 years ago. He thinks the apple trees always looked as they look today, which says something about how old they are.

He tells us about stealing apples from the teacher's garden during break, many years ago. Unfortunately he ran straight into the teacher, who asked him to help carry wood to the woodshed.

What else could he do but let go of the hold on his shirt under which the apples were hidden and grab hold of the basket!

All the apples rolled out on the ground. The teacher did not say anything - "but when the wood had been stacked, I was told to go out and fill up the empty basket with apples from the garden and to have the boy sitting next to me in class help carry it in — and then the apples were distributed among us all."

"That teacher was a great guy," he said.

The teacher's wife was a classic lady, who ran her house well, took care of her 10 children, invited guests in for coffee and apple pies.

She always used Danish Lemon apples and a variety that tastes of pineapples. She would peel them, divide them and core them and cook them gently to a nice apple sauce — just sweet enough.

She first separated 3 egg whites from their yolks. Then she would bake a crust made of

100 g (3½ oz) butter
100 g (3½ oz) sugar
100 g (3½ oz) corn flour
3 eggs yolks
1 teaspoon baking powder

She would stir it all together very thoroughly for a long time and would then take the saved egg whites, beaten stiff, and carefully blend them in.

The crust was placed on a platter and the apple sauce spread on top. Then she would make a delicious Lemon custard from

  1 egg
  1 dl (½ cup) cream
  1½ tablespoons sugar
  1 tablespoon flour

which she beat together while gently heating it up on the stove. Then she would add juice from ½ Lemon.

Finally she crushed little macaroons over the cake and then she decorated it with whipped cream. The teacher's wife had quite an artful hand.

Many duties are involved when running a house and garden and fruit trees.

Picking is very exciting. It must be done right. Every apple must be twisted off the twig, so the stem is not broken off. At the teacher's home everybody was involved.

Around harvest time mother would summon some of the girls to help peel apples, big style. In order to have dried apples, large trays with apple rings were placed in the sun. In this way a large supply of apples was created to go with the winter dishes of porridge, bacon and pork; And also for making Christmas candy.

The children loved

Apples On A String
and especially making them.

They would string apple rings on a cotton thread, dip them in a pancake dough and fry them golden in oil.

It was always the girls who were asked to peel apples, while the boys went on hayrides with the neighbor --- they said they were helping!

But the boys were in for it when they had to help their father pruning the fruit trees in winter.

It might be fun to cut and saw, but what made it a tedious job for them, was the knowledge their father considered his duty to teach them, about how and why the sawing and pruning had to be done in a certain way.

When Luise, the third born, celebrated her birthday late in July, the first apple dessert of the season was served. The first ripe summer apples were used — and when this dessert seemed to taste especially good, it was probably because it was the very first of the season — or perhaps because Luise's birthday party was always such a delightful event. Naturally the dessert was called

Luise's Birthday Cake

2½ cups flour
1½ cups sugar
125 g (1⅛ stick) butter
2 eggs
½ teaspoon baking powder
½ cup water

Mix it all together.

Peel, core and slice 6 apples. Grease a breadpan and then fill it with layers of apples and dough. Sprinkle with brown sugar and bake for 45 minutes at 360 °F.

In the good old days a piece of land belonged to the school. The teacher kept a couple of cows and of course some chickens. There was never a shortage of milk and eggs. The heavy cream that could be skimmed off the milk in the cellar was not a strain on the budget of the teacher's wife -she could afford to be generous — and whipped cream on top of the apple dessert gave it the finishing touch — as here on

The Good Old Danish

Peel, core and slice 10 apples and cook them slightly with ½ cup of water and 2½ tablespoons sugar. Mix 50 g (½ stick) butter, 85 g (⅓ cup) sugar and 125 g (4½ oz) breadcrumbs and roast it lightly in the frying pan. When cool, layer apples and breadcrumbs in a bowl and decorate with whipped cream and dots of red currant jelly.

When we visit with friends and are served slightly different versions of this good old *Danish Apple Charlotte*, we often think their dessert is especially good. The reason may be that everyone has their own unique way of creating it.

For instance Elizabeth. She conjures up her gorgeous dessert by adding homemade Cowberry jam between the layers. It is a delightful idea.

Else is all for rosehips. She decorates with lots of preserved and halved rosehips. They are full of C vitamins and look beautiful.

Gerda sprinkles her dessert with red glazed cherries and grated orange peel. It looks very festive and tastes great.

While I think of times gone by and old delicacies and all the efforts we made in order to create good results, I am right now making the easiest pie in the world. In all simplicity it goes like this:

Easy Pie
  ⅔ cup oil
  ⅓ cup milk
  2 cups flour

I stir or knead this dough directly into the ovenproof pie dish and press the dough up the edge of the dish.

I add thinly cut apple slices from 3 or 4 apples and sprinkle with a couple of tablespoons sugar and a little cinnamon.

I spread lumps of butter on top and bake for 20 minutes at 360 °F.

You can use different fruits from the garden for a filling and also cheese.

A couple of other pies can be made in a hurry:

The Fast One

Place a yellow layer cake in a
shallow dish. Cover it with apple
sauce and sprinkle crushed macaroons on top, then
whipped cream — uhm -

Chocolate Apple Dessert

Place a yellow layer cake in a shallow dish. Pour
a cup of raspberry juice over it. Then crush 5 small
macaroons and sprinkle on top, then apple sauce from
4 apples. Cover this with a store bought chocolate
custard (a crème powder does make life easier). If
you have rum in the house, do add a little.

Whipped cream on top — delicious -

Apple Slices

200 g (2 cups) flour
80 g (½ cup) sugar
1 egg
100 g (⅞ stick) butter

Mix to a dough and spread in a thin layer in a roasting pan. Sprinkle 12 crushed macaroons over it.

Peel, core and slice 10 apples and cook with 10 tablespoons sugar, (no water) in a covered saucepan over low heat for 15 minutes. Mash and spread over the dough. Then mix a new dough from:

200 g (2 cups) flour
200 g (1¾ stick) butter
150 g (¾ cup) sugar
3 eggs
1 teaspoon baking powder

Spoon this on top and spread out with a fork — that is the easiest way. Bake for 20 minutes at 425 $^{\circ}$F. When cool cut into many delicious slices.

You cannot own an apple tree — and certainly not an old apple tree — it belongs to itself.

But if there is one in your garden, you can enjoy belonging to its inner circle and accept what it generously produces.

We make an effort to reciprocate by giving attention and admiration and keeping an eye on what it may need.

If the summer has been dry and the following winter without snow and rain, the tree will be so thirsty that it must be watered. Through a homemade irrigation system many buckets of water may be poured down to the longing roots .

In case it has been attacked by vermin or disease it must be cured without doses of poison.

During May it presents its first gift, the flower show, so rich there is enough for a pink bouquet to put in the old vase.

It stretches a strong branch out over the lawn, perfect for holding a swing.

Year after year playful children have been spinning in the heavy ropes or pushed each other to weightlessness way high up in the air from where they could get a glimpse of the neighbor's trees and fields all the way to the Poplar fence.

Well, this old apple tree has seen a lot.

Its gnarled trunk has willingly lent itself to one more of the family members – the cat. He takes an obvious delight in sharpening his claws on the bark before he starts a wild climb up its gnarled challeging branches.

And what a relief for soul and body when on a hot summer's day it invites us to a place in the shade under its domed crown.

Some wonderful apples grow in Jutland. They are called Tyrrestrup Cherry Apples.

The grafting twig was long ago obtained from the Tyrrestrup Manor's nursery garden. Now these gorgeous apple trees represent East Jutland in the most honorable way. There are a few recipes with exactly these apples. but in case they are not available. apple varieties like Fillipa or any other tasty variety will do well.

Tyrrestrup Cherry Apple

The Tyrrestrup Cake

Peel, core and cut 6 apples into bits and
place them in a greased ovenproof dish with
½ cup water and 85 g (3 oz) sugar.

Mix together ½ cup corn oil
100 g (1 cup) flour
50 g (¼ cup) sugar

and pour over the apples — bake for about 20 minutes
at 360 °F. Serve with whipped cream.

Sunday Apples

Peel, core and cut 10 apples into small pieces and mix
into a dough made of

200 g (1¾ stick) butter
200 g (1 cup) sugar
100 g (¾ cup) breadcrumbs.

Place in an ovenproof dish and bake for 30 to
45 minutes at 400 °F. Serve with whipped
cream or lemon cream. (see page 7)

The Dannebrog Cake

Dannebrog is the name of the Danish flag. When my grandfather was knighted by the Danish king in 1928 and visited the school after this event, this cake was served.

The cake was made by his daughter-in-law, and his son gave him a nice speech. The children asked: "Grandfather, what is a Dannebrog's man?"

Peel, core and divide 5 apples and cook them lightly with ½ cup water and 5 tablespoons sugar. Place them on top of a yellow layer cake which will absorb all the juice.

Spread a good rum crème over it and cover it with another yellow layer cake. Decorate with red currant jelly and white meringues and it resembles the Danish flag.

The old school welcomes holiday guests.

A German friend came visiting — a real *Hausfrau* skilled at cooking and baking. When she saw the large Royal apples she burst out: "Oh, wie herrlich für Apfelkuchen." The next day she was in her element in the kitchen. She made

Prima Apfelkuchen

200 g (2 cups) flour
125 g (¾ cup) sugar
125 g (1⅛ stick) butter
3 eggs
2 teaspoons baking powder
juice of ½ lemon

Mix the dough and place in a flat ovenproof dish. Peel and core 5 apples and divide them into quarters. Place them on top of the dough, lightly scratch the surface and sprinkle sugar on top.

Bake for ca 40 minutes at 360°F.

Quark is not as common here as in parts of Europe.
It is a product made from curdled milk, strained into
soft white cheese, a fresh acid-set cheese which gives
a spongy, never dry consistency to baked goods.

Quark Buns

50 g (½ stick) butter
100 g (½ cup) sugar
50 g (2½ teaspoons) yeast
5 tablespoons milk
1 tablespoon vanilla
1 egg
200g (1 cup) Quark
200 g (2 cups) flour
200 g (2½ cups) small apple pieces
50 g (1 cup) raisins

Mix the ingredients and let rise for 30 minutes.

In a saucepan heat up ½ liter (½ quart) corn oil.
Cook spoonfuls of dough in the oil, remove with
perforated ladle and let dry on a wire tray.

Schubert Cake

100 g (1 cup) flour
100 g (¾ cup) cornflour
100 g (⅞ stick) butter
1 egg
1 teaspoon vanilla
65 g (¾ cup) sugar

Mix and bake in a springform or roasting pan for 15 minutes at 400 °F. Meanwhile stir together

100 g (⅞ stick) butter
100 g (½ cup) sugar
3 teaspoons vanilla
1 egg
400 g (1¾ cup) quark
75 g (¾ cup) corn flour
2 teaspoons baking powder
1 tablespoon raisins
⅛ liter (½ cup) cream
4 large apples, peeled, cored and diced.

Place this dough on top of the dough in the oven and continue baking for another 40 – 50 minutes at 380 °F

Heidi's Sunday Cake

125 g (1⅛ stick) butter
150 g (¾ cup) sugar
300 g (1½ cups) flour
2 eggs
4 tablespoons milk
juice from 1 lemon

Stir it all together and place in a springform pan. Peel and core 10 apples and cut them into halves, scratch the surface lightly and place them on the dough. Sprinkle with brown sugar and bake for 45 minutes at 350 °F. Serve with whipped cream.

Heidi always brings her Dirnlkleid (dress) when on vacation. She knows how to bake and also how to yodel.

John and Jim from England prefer their homeland's apple crumble. No apple dessert overshadows it! They showed us how to make it and gave us their recipe.

Apple Crumble

300 g (3 cups) flour
2oo g (1¾ stick) butter
100 g (½ cup) sugar
½ teaspoon salt

Judging by the name you almost know that the dough is neither kneaded nor stirred — no — it must be crumbled between your fingers, till it is almost pulverized.

Cut 6 apples into eighths and cook them lightly in water with a little sugar. Dry them on a paper towel and place in a greased ovenproof dish.

Pour 3 tablespoons Sherry over and cover with the dough. Add a few dots of butter on top. Bake at about 360 °F till golden brown. Serve it lukewarm with a sherry custard - great.

Just to stay with the outlandish! In Paris we were
once served an apple omelet. We brought the idea home
with us as a souvenir.

Apple Omelet de Paris

Beat 4 egg yolks with ½ cup milk, add 1 tablespoon flour,
   1 teaspoon cardamon
   1 teaspoon sugar
   ½ teaspoon salt
   and last the beaten egg whites

Make two omelettes. Put a good portion
of applesauce between them. Pour a glass of
cognac over. Sprinkle a little sugar on top and
serve with whipped cream — o la la.

French apple cakes are delicious. Here is a

French Apple Cake

Grease a large ovenproof dish and sprinkle the bottom
with breadcrumbs and then a layer of macaroons dipped
in corn oil. Peel, core and cut 6 apples into quarters
and cook them almost tender in water with a little sugar.

Let them dry off and then place half the portion in the dish. Cover with a layer of raspberry jam, then a layer of macaroons dipped in Madeira, then the rest of the apples and another layer of raspberry jam. Beat 3 egg yolks with ¾ cup cream and 1 tablespoon corn flour.

Add the whipped egg whites and pour over the dish. Sprinkle some breadcrumbs and sugar on top and bake for 30 minutes at 360 °F.

 # St. Michel Cake 

Cut 6 peeled and cored apples into squares and cook gently in 1½ dl (¾ cup) white wine and 3 tablespoons of sugar. Let them dry off and place them in an ovenproof dish. Pour on top a custard made with:

3 egg yolks
2 tablespoons sugar
2 tablespoons flour
3 dl (1¾ cup) milk
1 teaspoon vanilla

Beat the whites with 100 g (½ cup) sugar and spread over cake. Bake at 350 °F for 45 to 60 minutes till the meringue is light brown.

There is sometimes a "get together" at the vicarage, and all are welcome. Even though the minister's wife routinely arranges long tables for coffee parties, it happened once that so many people showed up they ran out of layer cakes. (Danish layer cakes are like Boston Cream Pies). That day the minister's wife quickly composed the

Snow Cake

She whipped ¼ liter (1 cup) cream while her maid grated 2 apples and mixed in 2 tablespoons confectioner's sugar. Apples and cream were blended and half of it was placed between two yellow layer cakes, the rest on top of them. It looked like a snow cake and became popular as such.
It tasted great.

Some apple desserts are equally suited for serving at the dinner table as at the coffee table.

Apple Gratin

Divide 8 peeled and cored apples into eighths. Roll them in 75 g (²⁄₃ cup) sugar and sprinkle them with juice from ½ lemon. Place in a greased ovenproof dish.

Beat 3 egg yolks with
75 g (²⁄₃ cup) sugar and stir in
2 tablespoons corn flour and
1 teaspoon cinnamon,
1 teaspoon vanilla and
½ l (2 cups) milk

Beat the three egg whites and fold them in carefully. Then pour over the apples and bake at 360 °F for about 30 minutes.

This recipe is from my grandmother's cookbook. She had added a little note: "Good, but expensive." Her recipe was for 24 people and it started: "Use 18 eggs." I have halved the recipe.

Aristocrat Cake

I use 9 eggs, but keep 7 of the egg whites separate. Stir the rest with 250 g (1¼ cup) sugar and 250 g (3 cups) ground almonds and finally add the beaten 7 whites. Pour half in a spring-form and bake for 30 minutes at ca 350 °F.

Cook pieces of 9 apples, peeled and cored, in sugar water. Let dry and place on the dough. Spread 3 tablespoons cherry jam on top and then the rest of the dough and bake for another 30 minutes.

Place on a platter and when cool decorate with a ring of meringues, and in the middle fill up with vanilla custard. (2 eggs, ¼ cup sugar, 40 g flour, ½ l milk, vanilla). And on top of that, believe it or not, whipped cream.

The Fancy One

Peel, core and cut into quarters 5 large
apples and steam them half tender in 50 g (¼
cup) sugar and 1 dl (½ cup) sherry. Place in an
ovenproof dish and cover with a dough made of

200 g (2 cups) flour
2oo g (7 oz) butter
50 g (¼ cup) sugar
3 dl (1½ cup) cream
6 egg yolks

Beat the egg whites well and add 100 g (½ cup)
sugar and 100 g (1 cup) ground almonds and spread
over the dough. Bake for about an hour at 360 °F.

It tastes so good warm. Place a bowl of whipped
cream on the table for those who may be tempted.

In the old days people were very frugal, but they knew how to have a good time.

On a winter's eve, when the stove indoors and the wind outside competed about rumbling, it was great to be able to fetch some large, tasty apples — with stem - from the cellar and place them to bake on the stove.

They would sizzle with a wonderful fragrance, and when done, each member of the family would place his apple on a saucer, sprinkle it with sugar while holding on to the stem and eat the tender, juicy apple with a teaspoon.

You can still do this today, if you have that kind of stove, but as time has gone by, some sophisticated recipes for baked apples have emerged.

Here are a few such recipes:

Brandy Apples

Take a suitable number of large apples and core them, but do not peel them. Into each apple pour 1 teaspoon sugar, 1 teaspoon cognac and some chopped walnuts. Place them in an ovenproof dish and bake at 360 °F for about 20 minutes. While baking add a little cognac a couple of times. Enjoy them warm with soft ice cream.

Apples And Dices

Cut three slices of white bread into cubes and brown them in corn oil in the frying pan. Remove them onto a plate and sprinkle with sugar and cinnamon.

Then add 6 apples - with the peel on and cut into quarters - into the frying pan together with a handful of raisins and one large tablespoon sugar.

Turn down the heat and place a lid over them. After 10 minutes they should be done.

Then spread the bread cubes on top and place the pan on the table.

A cold vanilla sauce goes well with this - and it is quite a dish for children and simple souls.

It is strange that this red, juicy apple is named after an exotic fruit that grows far from our land. It is called a Pine apple, maybe due to its aroma and sweet and sourly taste.

It is beautiful, a purple red, and how it shines, when you rub its skin!

You can hardly make yourself take a bite. But if on a normal weekday you feel like creating a festive mood, it is a great idea to bake this rose colored apple pancake. The Pine Apple has always been used for this.

Apple Pancake With Red Cheeks

Cut 4 – 6 red apples into halves, remove the core and make a few scratches in the skin.

Heat up plenty of corn oil in the frying pan and fry the apples on the red side for about 3 – 4 minutes. Carefully turn them over with a spatula and fry them 4 minutes more.

Make a pancake dough with 1 egg, 1 tablespoon flour, 1 dl (½ cup) milk, 1 teaspoon sugar and ½ teaspoon cardamon. Pour it in the frying pan without covering the apples. When done, sprinkle a spoonful of sugar over it.

Place it on the table with some powdered sugar for anyone who may want it.

Apple Dip

Place some apple slices, not too thin, in a mixture of sugar, cinnamon and cognac for about an hour. Make a pancake dough of 150 g (1½ cup) flour, 2 eggs, ½ cup milk, 1 tablespoon oil, ½ teaspoon salt, 1 teaspoon sugar and 2 tablespoons rum.

Remove the apples and pour the juice into the pancake dough. Then dip the apple slices in the dough and fry them golden brown in corn oil.

We enjoy apple dips with a drink, with tea, coffee or just for fun......

The worst thing about stir cakes is -they have to be stirred. At least that is what the teacher's children thought. They were always asked to do it.

It was tough to sit for an hour and stir and stir "always the same way round so as not to destroy the air bubbles", they were told.

If a handmixer had been known back then — what a bliss it would have been.

Stir cakes are popular and can be varied. Here are some, named and recommended by friends of the school.

Mimi's Apple Cake

125 g (1⅛ stick) butter
150 g (¾ cup) sugar
200 g (2 cups) flour
2 eggs — divided
½ teaspoon baking powder
2 tablespoons water

Mix all but the egg whites. They must be beaten and folded in last. Peel and core 3 apples and cut in small pieces. Place half the dough in an ovenproof dish, put the apples on top, and then the rest of the dough. Mix sugar with chopped orange peel and sprinkle on top. Bake for ca 45 minutes at 400 °F.

Ida's Carrot Cake

250 g flour, 100 g (½ cup) sugar, 1 dl (½ cup) oil, 1 teaspoon baking powder. Mix and add 200 g (7 oz) grated carrots and 200 g grated apples and juice from 1 lemon. Bake in roasting pan for 30 minutes at 400 °F.

Ulrik's Cake

Beat 6 eggs and mix in
- 300 g (1½ cup)sugar
- 300 g (2¾ sticks) butter
- 250 g (2¼ cup) flour
- 250 g (1¾ cup) corn flour
- 1 teaspoon baking powder
- 6 apples, cut into eighths
- 2 teaspoons cinnamon
- 1 teaspoon cardamon
- 1 teaspoon cloves
- 1 cup raisins

Bake at 400 °F for 45 – 60 minutes

Sven's Favorite

Beat 3 egg yolks with 100 g (½ cup) sugar, add 100 g (3½ oz) butter, 150 g (1½ cup) flour, 200 g quark, 2 teaspoons ginger, 1 teaspoon cinnamon, 2 teaspoons baking powder. Add 4 apples, cut into very small pieces. Place in an ovenproof dish. Beat stiff the 3 egg whites with ½ cup sugar and spread over the dough. Bake at 360 °F for about 30 minutes.

Olga's Apple Cake

4 eggs, the whites to be kept separate and
beaten to be added last.
250 g (2¼ sticks) butter
250 g (1¼ cups) sugar
250 g (2¼ cups) flour
1 teaspoon baking powder
2 teaspoons vanilla
3 large grated apples
50 g chopped almonds
Grated rind of 1 lemon

Bake for 45 minutes at 400 °F.

If you need to bake a really big cake there is

Maren's Mix

Beat 6 eggs with 250 g (2¼ cup) dark brown sugar,
250 g (2¼ stick) butter, 500 g (2½ cup) flour,
1 teaspoon baking powder, 50 g chopped walnuts, 3
tablespoons rum, 100 g (3½ oz) glazed cherries and
10 peeled and cored apples cut into pieces. Bake at
400 °F for about 60 minutes.

Jytte's Marzipan Cake

if you are crazy for something sweet….. Stir

3 eggs with

150 g (¾ cup) sugar

200 g (1¾ stick) butter

100 g (1 cup) flour

100 g (¾ cup) corn flour

2 teaspoons baking powder

Place in a greased bread pan. Then mix 100 g (3½ oz) marzipan with 4 tablespoons rum and press this in to a groove down the middle of the dough. Over that, a large tablespoon of raisins and pieces of apples from 3 – 4 peeled apples. Sprinkle with sugar and sliced almonds. Bake for ca 30 minutes at 400 °F.

The Fabulous Yeast Pretzel

Whether it has the shape of a pretzel or is round or oblong, the homemade yeast cake is almost a status symbol for the lady of the house.

A coffee party will never go wrong if you have a great recipe for a delicious yeast pretzel. Your guests will rave about it and help themselves to another piece.

Apples inside can add a fresh taste to different varieties of this pretzel.

Coffee Party Pretzel

400 g (4 cups) flour
200 g (1¾ sticks) butter
50 g (¼ cup) sugar
50 g (2½ teaspoons) yeast
a pinch of salt

Dissolve the yeast in a tablespoon water and the sugar. Mix it all together to a nice dough and spread it over a baking sheet. Then mix 75 g (⅔ stick) butter and 75 g (⅓ cup) sugar and smear it down the middle of the dough. Cover with two finely sliced apples, 5 crushed macaroons and two tablespoons black currant wine. Fold the sides up well. The cake may be open, but it is wise to support the sides with baking paper so the content will not run out onto the sheet.

Let the pretzel rise for 30 minutes, then brush with egg and sprinkle with sugar and chopped almonds.

Bake for 30 minutes at 370 °F

Apple Pie with Orange

200 g (2 cups) flour
100 g (3½ oz) butter
1 tablespoon of milk
1 tablespoon of sugar
25 g yeast (1½ teaspoons)
1 egg

Dissolve the yeast in milk and sugar and work in the rest. Place ⅔ of the dough in a pie dish, well up the edges to contain the filling. Blend 50 g (½ stick) butter with 50 g (¼ cup) sugar and add 40 g chopped orange peel.

First smear the filling over the dough, then add 3 finely sliced apples. Cut the last third of the dough into ribbons and decorate across the pie.

Brush the pie with milk and sprinkle with sugar. Let rise 30 minutes, then bake at 400 °F for 20 minutes.

A Spicy Pretzel

500 g (4½ cup) flour
50 g (½ stick) butter
200 g (1 cup) brown sugar
50 g (2½ teaspoons) yeast
3 eggs
2 dl (1 cup) milk
1 teaspoon cardamon
1 teaspoon cinnamon
1 teaspoon cloves
1 teaspoon ginger
a handful raisins
4 large apples cut into pieces.

Mix it all well and this time shape the dough into a real old fashioned pretzel and brush it with egg and sprinkle it with sugar and chopped almonds.

Let it rise 45 minutes, then bake for 30 minutes at 400 °F.

An Apple Loaf

The teacher's two youngest daughters once introduced an apple loaf. Admittedly their first edition was hard and charred when it emerged from the spirit flame in the dollhouse stove. But it probably never tasted better.

It is a good idea. A buttered slice of Apple Loaf with the filling inside is a real treat.

500 g (4½ cup) flour, 25 g (¼ stick) butter, 2 dl (1 cup) water, 50 g (¼ cup) sugar, salt, 5 apples cut into eighths.

Let rise and bake just like a loaf of bread.

Puff Paste

These days it is easy to bake with puff paste since it can be bought frozen. And since there is only one recipe for puff paste, the homemade and the store bought are equally good.

 Puff Paste Cake with Apples 

Place 4 sheets of puff paste on a baking sheet and press together so they become one long piece of dough.

Cook pieces of 4 apples in sugar water and dry off, then place on the dough. Sprinkle with cinnamon and sugar.

Then cover with a layer of 4 more sheets of puff paste.

Squeese edges and openings together with moist fingers, so the filling will not run out.

If you want to be fancy, use a fork on the edges.

Brush with egg and sprinkle with sugar and bake in a hot oven about 15 minutes.

Surprises

The recipe is old and was originally made according to directions which included cooling down and rolling out many times. Today it is easy. We just grab a package of frozen puff paste and cut the oblong pieces of dough in half.

On each square of dough we place a slice of marzipan and top it with a slice of apple. Fold it together to a triangle and close it with moist fingers. Bake it at 360 °F to 400 °F for about 10 minutes. The finished triangles look very festive when decorated with icing sugar in different colors, for instance a yellow with lemon flavor, a red with strawberry flavor, a brown with chocolate flavor and a white with peppermint flavor.

When the trees stand like silhouettes against the winter sky and the snow covers all that is edible, the birds become an important part on the daily agenda.

The blackbird who sings so well loves apples. And during the winter months we regularly have to go through our different sorts of apples as they do not all keep well.

This means apples for the birds. The blackbird is a good eater and loves his daily meals.

The October Cake

It is practical to store some short crust pastry in your cake tin. It will make it easy to put a cake together. Place one in a pie dish and moisten it with 2 tablespoons Grand Marnier. Cover with apple sauce from 4 apples and a little lemon juice and grate two apples on top of this, and then sprinkle with a large tablespoon sugar and a handful chopped hazel nuts.

Bake about 15 minutes in a hot oven.

Pour another spoonful of Grand Marnier over it and serve with whipped cream.

And it is exciting to go nut picking.

The Potato Apple Cake

Grate 500 g (1 pound) boiled potatoes and mix with 125 g ($1\frac{1}{8}$ stick) melted butter. Stir 6 egg yolks with 200 g (1 cup) sugar and add grated rind and juice from one lemon. Add 2 big cups of apple pieces and the potatoes and finally fold in the 6 whipped egg whites. Bake in an ovenproof dish for about 1 hour at 360 °F.

An Apple Pyramid

can look very impressive, but it is hardly what you will put on an elegant table when serving coffee at a banquet. Rather you will enjoy doing this with the children.

Mix 400 g (4/5 pound) syrup with $\frac{1}{3}$ liter (¾ cup) water, then heat it up and cook small red apples in it and arrange them into a grand pyramid. Pour any leftover syrup on the pyramid and serve with cookies.

Walnut Apple Cake

Peel, core and slice 5 large apples and place in an ovenproof dish. Add the juice of ½ lemon and 3 tablespoons sugar. Bake in a warm oven for 15 minutes. Meanwhile stir together

75 g (⅔ stick) butter
50 g (¼ cup) sugar
1 egg
50 g chopped walnuts

and cover the apples with this. Bake for 10 more minutes. Serve with whipped cream or custard.

Rice Cake

If you have some left over from dinner use that, otherwise make rice porridge from ½ liter (2½ cup) milk and 25 g rice. Place in an ovenproof dish. Add 4 apples, cut into quarters and 2 tablespoons strawberry jam. Then cover with a large cup thick vanilla custard and 3 crushed macaroons. Bake about 20 minutes at 360 °F This is a very old recipe.

At the end of the garden grows a tree with apples of an unknown kind. The apples are hard and sour, but they stay on the tree long after the frost has killed whatever else was beautiful in the garden. We call it the Sjagger tree.

Every year the Sjaggers, the beautiful birds from the North, come and settle in the tree and start eating the fruit. The birds — the golden apples — the snowclad garden — a more beautiful sight on a dark winter's day you will never see. The tree always has an abundance of fruits, and some years at the end of the season we may use a few Sjagger apples and bake this

Sjagger Cake

Cut 2 pounds apples including peel and core into quarters and cook in a cup of water, then press through a sieve. Add 100 g (½ cup} sugar and thicken with 4 sheets (2 teaspoons) of gelatin and place in a bowl. Cover with 1 cup breadcrumbs and top with vanilla custard. Cool in fridge.

Christmas starts the 1st of December, when first the advent decorations come out. In our home it is an indestructible wrought iron candlestick that holds 4 candles.

It has 4 spikes on which can sit some red apples, and the small red pigeon apples are perfect for it.

It is a wonderful feeling to start decorating the advent candlestick as the start of Christmas -and to collect green spruce branches and rub the red apples till they shine.

The Advent Sundays are warm and cosy days.

The long, dark winter days can be perfect for finishing tasks at home. We can also bake a cake, for instance a

 # Pigeon Apple Cake 

Mix 1 cup small pieces of Pigeon Apples with the rind on in 2 tablespoons oil and 2 tablespoons sugar and boil for a short while. Then stir together

3 tablespoons flour
1 tablespoon sugar
1 tablespoon oil
1 tablespoon water
1 egg

Place the apple pieces in an ovenproof dish and crumble the dough on top, then sprinkle some breadcrumbs over. Put 6 half pigeon apples on top, prick them and sprinkle sugar over and bake about 20 minutes at 400 °F.

Coconut Apples

Make a dough of 200 g (2 cups) flour

150 g (1½ cup) corn flour
150 g (¾ cup) sugar
1½ dl (¾ cup) corn oil
4 egg yolks
2 teaspoons baking powder

and spread it in a roasting pan. Peel and core 6 apples and cut them into halves and place them on the dough. Whip the 4 egg whites with 150 g (¾ cup sugar), add 150 g (¾ cup) coconut flour and distribute over the apples. Bake for about 45 minutes at 340 °F.

Christmas is the season for gifts — here is a suggestion

Apple Packages

250 g (2 cups) flour
200 g (1 cup) Quark
100 g (⅞ stick) butter
1 teaspoon salt
2 teaspoons sugar
1 teaspoon baking powder

Peel and core 4 apples and fill them with chopped nuts and sugar. Roll out the dough and divide it into 4 portions. On each portion place a filled apple and wrap it carefully. Moisten the edges of the dough and squeeze them together. Brush the packages with egg, sprinkle with sugar and bake at 360 °F. approximately 20 minutes till they are golden brown.

Upside-Down Cake

Peel and core 5 apples and cut into mall pieces and mix with 100 g (½ cup) sugar and 150 g (1 cup) chopped almonds. Put into a springform well greased and coated with breadcrumbs. Cover the apples with a dough of

75 g (⅔ stick) butter
150 g (¾ cup) sugar
1 egg
125 g (1½ cup) flour
75 g (2⅔ oz) corn flour
1 pinch salt
1 small cup milk
2 teaspoons baking powder

Bake at 360 °F. for about 45 minutes. When the cake is done, open the springform pan and remove the side, and when the cake has been turned around so the apples are on top, remove the bottom. When cool the cake is ready to be decorated with whipped cream, red currant jelly, almonds, hearts and gnomes.

When we talk about Christmas and apples, we must not forget one of the oldest Christmas traditions, the Æbleskiver. Originally the apple was the essential part, now it is the dough.

This recipe is from an old cookbook - when people measured in quarts and gills, lump and tub, and when a slice of apple was just that. Here it is:

Whip 5 eggs together with

¼ liter (1⅓ cup) cream
⅛ liter (¾ cup) water
¼ liter (1⅓ cup) melted butter
¼ liter (1½ cup) flour

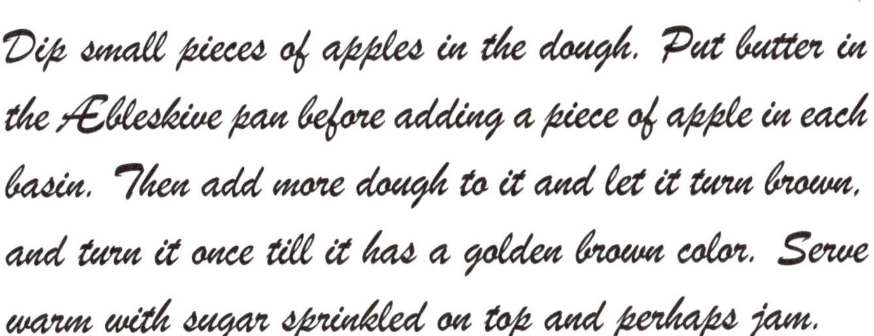

Dip small pieces of apples in the dough. Put butter in the Æbleskive pan before adding a piece of apple in each basin. Then add more dough to it and let it turn brown, and turn it once till it has a golden brown color. Serve warm with sugar sprinkled on top and perhaps jam.

The frugal housewife invented this New Year cake. It is quite simply a 'recycle' cake. There is always some oil left over when finished baking Klejner. Klejner is a Danish fried cookie made at Christmas time. We always use Corn oil for this.

The New Year Cake

250 g (2½ cup) flour
250 g (1¼ cup) sugar
2 eggs
2 dl (1 cup) oil
1 teaspoon baking powder
pinch of favorite spice
5 apples
150 g (6 Oz) candied cherries

Cut 5 apples, peeled and cored, into quarters. Dip them in some of the flour and fry in oil in a frying pan. Mix the rest of the ingredients and combine it all.

Then put everything in a bread pan and bake for about 60 minutes at 360 °F.

This is a very easy cake to slice, and it has become a tradition. Friends who come visiting at the school most certainly expect to be treated to a piece together with Glögg or Toddy, when they come to wish us Happy New Year after a brisk long walk.

Index